T0346827

A CENTURY *of*
THE POTTERIES

Advertisement for Buffalo Bill's Wild West Show in Stoke, 1904.

A CENTURY *of* THE POTTERIES

ALAN TAYLOR

First published in the United Kingdom in 2000 by Sutton Publishing

This new paperback edition first published in 2007 by Sutton Publishing

Reprinted in 2008 by
The History Press
The Mill, Brimscombe Port,
Stroud, Gloucestershire, GL5 2QG
www.thehistorypress.co.uk

Reprinted 2010, 2011, 2012

British Library Cataloguing in Publication Data
A catalogue record for this book is available from the British Library.

ISBN 978-0-7509-4899-9

Front endpaper: Hospital Saturday, Audley, 1904.
Back endpaper: The Potteries Shopping Centre, Hanley, 1995.
Half title page: The water tower at the Michelin works.
Title page: Sponging at Johnson's works, 1989.

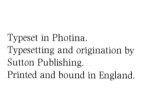

For Jan, Josh and Sam

Typeset in Photina.
Typesetting and origination by
Sutton Publishing.
Printed and bound in England.

1908 Four nurses pose at the City General Hospital. They wear uniforms typical of the Edwardian period with starched collars and cuffs.

Contents

1917 Albert Edward Shaw was born in the family home above their newsagents shop in Etruria Vale Road. The business started during the First World War and Albert is seen wearing a three-quarter length dress. This was common attire for a young boy at the time.

Britain: A Century of Change

Two women encumbered with gas masks go about their daily tasks during the early days of the war. (*Hulton Getty Picture Collection*)

The sixty years ending in 1900 were a period of huge transformation for Britain. Railway stations, post-and-telegraph offices, police and fire stations, gasworks and gasometers, new livestock markets and covered markets, schools, churches, football grounds, hospitals and asylums, water pumping stations and sewerage plants totally altered the urban scene, and the country's population tripled with more than seven out of ten people being born in or moving to the towns. The century that followed, leading up to the Millennium's end in 2000, was to be a period of even greater change.

When Queen Victoria died in 1901, she was measured for her coffin by her grandson Kaiser Wilhelm, the London prostitutes put on black mourning and the blinds came down in the villas and terraces spreading out from the old town centres. These centres were reachable by train and tram, by the new bicycles and still newer motor cars, were connected by the new telephone, and lit by gas or even electricity. The shops may have been full of British-made cotton and woollen clothing but the grocers and butchers were selling cheap Danish bacon, Argentinian beef, Australasian mutton and tinned or dried fish and fruit from Canada, California and South Africa. Most of these goods were carried in British-built-and-crewed ships burning Welsh steam coal.

As the first decade moved on, the Open Spaces Act meant more parks, bowling greens and cricket pitches. The First World War transformed the place of women, as they took over many men's jobs. Its other legacies were the war memorials which joined the statues of Victorian worthies in main squares round the land. After 1918 death duties and higher taxation bit hard, and a quarter of England changed hands in the space of only a few years.

The multiple shop – the chain store – appeared in the high street: Sainsburys, Maypole, Lipton's, Home & Colonial, the Fifty Shilling Tailor, Burton, Boots, W.H. Smith. The shopper was spoilt for choice, attracted by the brash fascias and advertising hoardings for national brands like Bovril, Pears Soap, and Ovaltine. Many new buildings began to be seen, such as garages, motor showrooms, picture palaces (cinemas), 'palais de dance', and ribbons of 'semis' stretched along the roads and new bypasses and onto the new estates nudging the green belts.

During the 1920s cars became more reliable and sophisticated as well as commonplace, with developments like the electric self-starter making them easier for women to drive. Who wanted to turn a crank handle in the new short skirt? This was, indeed, the electric age as much as the motor era. Trolley buses, electric trams and trains extended mass transport and electric light replaced gas in the street and the home, which itself was groomed by the vacuum cleaner.

A major jolt to the march onward and upward was administered by the Great Depression of the early 1930s. The older British industries

– textiles, shipbuilding, iron, steel, coal – were already under pressure from foreign competition when this worldwide slump arrived. Luckily there were new diversions to alleviate the misery. The 'talkies' arrived in the cinemas; more and more radios and gramophones were to be found in people's homes; there were new women's magazines, with fashion, cookery tips and problem pages; football pools; the flying feats of women pilots like Amy Johnson; the Loch Ness Monster; cheap chocolate and the drama of Edward VIII's abdication.

Things were looking up again by 1936 and new light industry was booming in the Home Counties as factories struggled to keep up with the demand for radios, radiograms, cars and electronic goods, including the first television sets. The threat from Hitler's Germany meant rearmament, particularly of the airforce, which stimulated aircraft and aero engine firms. If you were lucky and lived in the south, there was good money to be earned. A semi-detached house cost £450, a Morris Cowley £150. People may have smoked like chimneys but life expectancy, since 1918, was up by 15 years while the birth rate had almost halved.

In some ways it is the little memories that seem to linger longest from the Second World War: the kerbs painted white to show up in

A W.H. Smith shop front in Beaconsfield, 1922.

the blackout, the rattle of ack-ack shrapnel on roof tiles, sparrows killed by bomb blast. The biggest damage, apart from London, was in the south-west (Plymouth, Bristol) and the Midlands (Coventry, Birmingham). Postwar reconstruction was rooted in the Beveridge Report which set out the expectations for the Welfare State. This, together with the nationalisation of the Bank of England, coal, gas, electricity and the railways, formed the programme of the Labour government in 1945.

Times were hard in the late 1940s, with rationing even more stringent than during the war. Yet this was, as has been said, 'an innocent and well-behaved era'. The first let-up came in 1951 with the Festival of Britain and there was another fillip in 1953 from the Coronation, which incidentally gave a huge boost to the spread of TV. By 1954 leisure motoring had been resumed but the Comet – Britain's best hope for taking on the American aviation industry – suffered a series of mysterious crashes. The Suez debacle of 1956 was followed by an acceleration in the withdrawal from Empire, which had begun in 1947 with the Independence of India. Consumerism was truly born with the advent of commercial TV and most homes soon boasted washing machines, fridges, electric irons and fires.

The *Lady Chatterley* obscenity trial in 1960 was something of a straw in the wind for what was to follow in that decade. A collective loss of inhibition seemed to sweep the land, as the Beatles and the Rolling Stones transformed popular music, and retailing, cinema and the theatre were revolutionised. Designers, hairdressers, photographers and models moved into places vacated by an Establishment put to flight by the new breed of satirists spawned by *Beyond the Fringe* and *Private Eye*.

In the 1970s Britain seems to have suffered a prolonged hangover after the excesses of the previous decade. Ulster, inflation and union troubles were not made up for by entry into the EEC, North Sea Oil, Women's Lib or, indeed, Punk Rock. Mrs Thatcher applied the corrective in the

Children collecting aluminium to help the war effort, London, 1940s. (*IWM*)

A street party to celebrate the Queen's Coronation, June 1953. (*Hulton Getty Picture Collection*)

1980s, as the country moved more and more from its old manufacturing base over to providing services, consulting, advertising, and expertise in the 'invisible' market of high finance or in IT.

The post-1945 townscape has seen changes to match those in the worlds of work, entertainment and politics. In 1952 the Clean Air Act served notice on smogs and pea-souper fogs, smuts and blackened buildings, forcing people to stop burning coal and go over to smokeless sources of heat and energy. In the same decade some of the best urban building took place in the 'new towns' like Basildon, Crawley, Stevenage and Harlow. Elsewhere open warfare was declared on slums and what was labelled inadequate, cramped, back-to-back, two-up, two-down, housing. The new 'machine for living in' was a flat in a high-rise block. The architects and planners who promoted these were in league with the traffic engineers, determined to keep the motor car moving whatever the price in multi-storey car parks, meters, traffic wardens and ring roads. The old pollutant, coal smoke, was replaced by petrol and diesel exhaust, and traffic noise.

Fast food was no longer only a pork pie in a pub

Punk rockers demonstrate their anarchic style during the 1970s. (*Barnaby's Picture Library*)

or fish-and-chips. There were Indian curry houses, Chinese take-aways and American-style hamburgers, while the drinker could get away from beer in a wine bar. Under the impact of television the big Gaumonts and Odeons closed or were rebuilt as multi-screen cinemas, while the palais de dance gave way to discos and clubs.

From the late 1960s the introduction of listed buildings and conservation areas, together with the growth of preservation societies, put a brake on 'comprehensive redevelopment'. The end of the century and the start of the Third Millennium see new challenges to the health of towns and the wellbeing of the nine out of ten people who now live urban lives. The fight is on to prevent town centres from dying, as patterns of housing and shopping change, and edge-of-town supermarkets exercise the attractions of one-stop shopping. But as banks and department stores close, following the haberdashers, greengrocers, butchers and ironmongers, there are signs of new growth such as farmers' markets, and corner stores acting as pick-up points where customers collect shopping ordered on-line from web sites.

Futurologists tell us that we are in stage two of the consumer revolution: a shift from mass consumption to mass customisation driven by

Millennium celebrations over the Thames
at Westminster, New Year's Eve, 1999.
(*Barnaby's Picture Library*)

a desire to have things that fit us and our particular lifestyle exactly,
and for better service. This must offer hope for small city-centre shop
premises, as must the continued attraction of physical shopping,
browsing and being part of a crowd: in a word, 'shoppertainment'.
Another hopeful trend for towns is the growth in the number of young
people postponing marriage and looking to live independently, alone,
where there is a buzz, in 'swinging single cities'. Theirs is a 'flats-and-
cafés' lifestyle, in contrast to the 'family suburbs', and certainly fits in
with government's aim of building 60 per cent of the huge amount of
new housing needed on 'brown' sites, recycled urban land. There looks
to be plenty of life in the British town yet.

The Potteries: An Introduction

To the outside world Stoke-on-Trent is known as the Potteries because of its traditional industry. The name of the city is known around the world because of the fine wares produced by the industry over the centuries. The scene has changed considerably over the last hundred years and the city is responding to the demands not only of its own citizens but also of the outside world.

At the turn of the twentieth century Britain was at war in South Africa. Many local men found themselves in a foreign country, fighting in a war they did not understand, defending the empire. The century was to be one of conflict, the war zones moving ever closer to the city during the Second World War. Stoke was fortunate in some ways. It did not suffer the devastation of Coventry, Manchester and Liverpool although bombers did target strategic points on which to unload their excess bombs as they returned from raids further north.

The pottery industry has changed considerably over the last hundred years. Gone now are the smoky bottle ovens that used to dominate the skyline and ruin the health of the people. A series of government measures to clean up the atmosphere has been successful. The industry

The North Stafford Hotel was opened in 1849 and along with the railway station buildings opposite, provides one of the more interesting examples of Victorian architecture.

turned from fossil fuels to electricity to fire the kilns and the economics of the industry have shifted production to other parts of the world in addition to Stoke. Rationalisation has resulted in smaller workforces and redundant potters have turned to other employment or set up their own businesses.

The other two major industries have also vanished. The reason why the pottery industry established itself in the North Staffordshire region was not so much the clay as the vast deposits of high quality coal. The kilns, growing in number from the eighteenth century onwards as pottery moved from a home-based craft to a factory organised industry, demanded huge quantities of coal. The fields around Stoke met the demand and exported the excess. Spoil heaps the size of small mountains leapt up all over the Potteries and were only later to be utilised for the public benefit by land redevelopment or the creation of recreational areas. That, however, was after the coal industry generally, not just in the Potteries, had been systematically destroyed. There are now no working pits in the region. Even the mining museum that had been set up at the Chatterley Whitfield colliery has gone. Smaller local initiatives to preserve this piece of the city's heritage are under way at the time of writing.

By the turn of the new millennium the steel industry too had gone. Shelton Bar works, originally the works set up by Earl Granville (1773–1846), had employed thousands of people both as a private business and, from 1952, as a nationalised industry. Innovations such as the unique horizontal charging of the blast furnaces had put the works at the forefront of the industry in this country. The city paid the price for this development. Standing next to Wedgwood's Etruria works, the two blighted the environment creating a huge stretch of wasteland. This was only recently cleared for the Garden Festival of 1986. A swathe of land was turned over to a series of gardens. The show was designed to encourage investment in Stoke and resulted in the Festival Park retail area which now combines recreational facilities such as Waterworld and

Prince's Road, Hartshill. The village of Hartshill attracted more wealthy residents seeking to escape the less healthy areas within the Potteries.

Trent Vale. The impact of large-scale extraction from the ground within the city can be clearly seen in this image.

Wedgwood's own former residence at Etruria Hall, now a hotel, with numerous businesses. This has had a detrimental effect on the town centres, drawing vast numbers of shoppers away from the traditional high streets and markets. It has also resulted in the closure of many cinemas as a multi-screen complex caters for the majority of tastes.

The city has maintained a sense of cultural diversity. Large numbers of people from around the globe have settled in North Staffordshire. The Irish and Welsh communities developed with the demand for labourers to build first the canals and then the railways. People seeking refuge from persecution in other parts of Europe and from the Far East have also settled in Stoke. The traditional view of the six towns is that they are extremely parochial: the residents of one never identify with the other towns. This culture persists but will probably dissolve with the ever growing means of communication now available to everybody. The increasing use of mobile phones, access to the internet and the growth in car ownership indicate a population reaching across those traditional boundaries.

The communication network has altered considerably over the twentieth century. The city benefited from an extensive railway network that carried both passengers and freight. This was broken up in the later part of the century, most of the land lying derelict for a number of years. The trackways have since been built over or reclaimed for recreational uses but the railways are fondly remembered. People travelled to their annual holidays on the trains, be it for a day out at Trentham Gardens, Rudyard Lake or Alton Towers, or further afield to Southport, Blackpool or the North Wales coast. These were the traditional seaside holiday resorts for Potters.

It has to be said that the health of the people in Stoke has suffered considerably because of the industry. At the turn of the twentieth century the majority of deaths followed lung-related diseases and the local hospitals concentrated on providing relief for illnesses such as asthma, TB and lung cancer. As the air was improved from the 1950s onwards, heart-related diseases and cancers of various types have become more prevalent.

Not represented in this book are some of the famous people associated with Stoke. Perhaps the most significant is Reginald Mitchell, designer of the Spitfire. Born at Butt Lane, his work took him away from the area at an early age in his tragically short life. His contribution of an aircraft that was to shape the future of the war and of aero-design should not be overlooked. Other local celebrities include Sir Oliver Lodge who invented the spark plug, instrumental in the development of the internal combustion engine; Lord Cadman who was responsible for shaping the future of the British oil industry; and of course Sir Stanley Matthews who inspired the postwar generations of football fans and players with his definitive skills. More recently, the city lays claim to being the home town of Robbie Williams and Nick Hancock. The place of Captain Edward Smith remains ambiguous for many people. A local man from lowly surroundings, he worked first as a Nasmyth hammer operator at Shelton Bar before following his half-brother to Liverpool and pursuing a career at sea. His skills as a mariner were matched by his social skills and he became the top commander of the White Star Line fleet. It was Smith who took the *Titanic* on her maiden voyage and the rest is history.

Many images in this book are being printed for the first time. I have sourced material from people outside the 'normal channels' hoping that this will make the book a more 'person-centred' work. These are the images of the area that people retain in their memories; these are day-to-day attempts at capturing a moment in time. The twentieth century was one in which the traditional structures in society were broken down, allowing the majority of people a voice of sorts and the opportunity, more than at any other time in history, to record something of themselves and their families.

Children play on the remains of a locomotive turned into a landcape feature on Scotia Road. Much of the industrial heritage of the city has found a similar fate. (*Courtesy of Denis Thorpe, The Guardian*)

The New City

1900 All Saints church, London Road, Boothen. Methodism has traditionally been the strongest Christian denomination in the Potteries since the eighteenth century. Many of the Anglican churches were rebuilt during the 1800s by the Church Commissioners. Parishes were redefined to take into account the huge demographic changes taking place in Stoke-on-Trent. All Saints was designed by Lynam and Rickman and built between 1887 and 1888. The Gothic styling is typical of the desire to provide high quality places of worship with a form of architectural pedigree.

1900 Charles Lamb and Fanny Locket were married. The photograph was taken soon after their wedding and presented in the style of a *carte de visite*, a form that had been hugely popular during the late nineteenth century. The desire to have a portrait taken, and for the status that conveyed, continued to grow.

1900 The twentieth century opened with Britain engaged in the Boer War in South Africa. Trooper Robert Beswick died at Howick, Natal on Christmas Day, 1900 at the age of twenty-two. He died of typhus fever that he caught from drinking contaminated water. Beswick served with the 6th Company 4th Battalion 8th Division of the Staffordshire Imperial Yeomanry as an advance scout and was highly regarded by his colleagues. A memorial was erected in his honour in the New Primitive Methodist church, Stone Road, Longton in 1901. Upon the demolition of the church in 1979 the memorial was rescued and eventually reinstated in Longton Town Hall in 1993. His father was James Wright Beswick, a pottery manufacturer who also served on the Longton Borough Council and later on the Stoke-on-Trent Borough Council. The family, including Robert, lived in Belgrave House in Dresden (a part of Longton).

1900 The Cobridge Royal Army Medical Corps.

1900 At the turn of the new century local transport depended on the roads and on horse-drawn vehicles. This wagon and team of horses belonged to the Trentham estate and they are seen here on the estate's weigh-bridge by Peacock Cottages in Park Drive.

1900 Longton Town Hall. A speaker addresses a small gathering outside the seat of Longton's Borough Council. Interestingly the first floor windows are glazed – in later images they appear blocked in with stone.

1900 Potbanks are mostly remembered for their characteristic bottle ovens. Most of the buildings are functional, developing in shape and size according to need. Some however, attempted to distinguish themselves as something above the ordinary. Enoch Wood's works in Burslem featured a crenellated entrance and this view of the Hill Pottery, also in Burslem, illustrates a strong Venetian influence.

901 The shop front of A. Harper on Victoria Road, Fenton. The shop was built in 1880 and in the window can be seen lampshades and gas mantles. There was heavy investment in gas supplies throughout the Potteries in the late nineteenth and early twentieth centuries. The British Gaslight Company, a London based business, supplied many parts of the area and successfully beat off local competition in the 1860s by temporarily lowering its high charges. During the 1870s Stoke borough Council and Fenton Local Board jointly regulated the gas supply. In 1904 the borough council opened an electricity works that was taken over by the county borough in 1910. Fenton, however, did not receive a general electricity supply until 1923. (*Courtesy of Jazz*)

1902 A view along Stafford Street, now The Strand, in Longton. The tram was the main form of public transport and one is seen here almost surrounded by carts pulled by horses. On the right of the picture the pawnbroker's sign hangs high, catching the eye. A little lower down the road a sign locates a public telephone.

1903 In the autumn of 1896 the great English composer, Edward Elgar, premiered *King Olaf* at the Victoria Hall in Hanley. It was a momentous occasion, the piece being described in *The Times* of 30 October as 'a work of high importance'. Elgar enjoyed the Victoria Hall, claiming the acoustics to be among the best in the land. Both the composer and his wife were well disposed towards the people of the Potteries. In a personal letter to Dora Mary Penny dated 18 March 1903, Elgar's wife described the local people as warm hearted. Penny was a close family friend. Her father, Alfred, had returned to serve as curate of Stoke-on-Trent in 1889 after a spell as a missionary in the Far East. He later served as vicar in Tunstall. Dora was identified as *Dorabella*, Variation 10 in Elgar's masterpiece.

1904 The entrance to the Cripples' Guild in Hanley. The Guild was the brainchild of the Duchess of Sutherland. In these buildings children were taught simple craft skills.

1904 A view of the old town hall in Hanley across Fountain Square. The local authority operated in these buildings from 1845 until the former Queen's Hotel superseded them in the 1880s. Lloyds Bank took over the building, with its heavy classical influence, in 1886, demolishing it and rebuilding on the site in 1936. To the rear of the building was Bee & Co., a carpet retailer.

1904 Before the outbreak of war in 1914, the North Staffordshire Infirmary and Eye Hospital was supported by voluntary donations. Each year the community at Audley held a 'Hospital Saturday'. Adults and children alike turned out in their best clothes or in fancy dress. Prize bands, the Boys' Brigade and the Church Lads' Brigade took part in the procession which also included decorated carts. Girls would take baskets filled with buttonholes and nosegays among the crowds from the stall held by the Hospital Committee at the church wall.

1905 A cookery class at school. In 1899 the school leaving age had been raised to twelve years but by 1900 there was already a strong feeling that this was not enough. Britain's industrial and commercial dominance was being challenged and the need for a literate and educated workforce was obvious. Under the 1902 Balfour Act, county councils and county borough councils were empowered to abolish school boards and set up local education authorities.

1905 Rudyard Lake proved to be a popular destination for day trippers from the Potteries. The North Staffordshire Railway Company ran a line to the Lake where boat trips and walking were favourite pastimes.

1905 While cheap terraced housing and factories were being built at an alarming rate throughout the six towns during the early years of the century, the surrounding area remained distinctly rural. Even today, Stoke-on-Trent has one of the few city centres from which open countryside can be reached within about ten minutes drive. Typical of the housing in these outlying rural areas are these cottages at Cellarhead. (*Courtesy of Cooper-Blore*)

1905 The memorial to Thomas Hulme, 1830–1905. Hulme was an earthenware manufacturer from Burslem. He also served as mayor for the town on two occasions. Like many of the pottery manufacturers, he was an active Methodist. He served as the organist at the Hill Top Sunday school for forty years. He also helped to compile the Methodist Free Church Tune Book in 1893. It was Hulme who gave the land for the new school of art in Burslem in 1904 which is one of the town's gems. Standing in Queen Street, it was designed by A.R. Wood and completed in 1907. The symmetry is finished in red brick and yellow terracotta. Hulme's monument reflects his standing and his aspirations. Both the Hill Top chapel and the Wedgwood Memorial Institute are illustrated.

1906 Trentham Hall. The Italianate splendour of the Hall is seen here as a backdrop to the terraced gardens. Ironically it has been the gardens that have become the legacy of the Sutherland family and can still be enjoyed today. The Hall was demolished in 1911/12.

909 Millicent Sutherland-Leveson-Gower, Duchess of Sutherland (1867–1955). seen with her daughter Rosemary. Millicent as one of the most remarkable women of her day. A noted society beauty, she used her privileged position at Trentham to influence attitudes towards the care of children in the Potteries area. She founded the Potteries Cripples' Guild in 1900 and established a partnership with Dame Agnes Hunt who had set up an open air hospital at Baschurch in Shropshire. Potteries children were sent to Baschurch until Millicent set up a similar establishment at Trentham. In 1909 this merged with the Cripples' Guild to form the North Staffordshire Cripples' Aid Society. Its home at Hanchurch was moved to Stoke before finding a permanent location at Hartshill at the end of the war in 1918. Among her other achievements, Millicent influenced the introduction of restrictions on the use of lead in the pottery industry – poisoning was one of the major causes of death and serious illness, particularly among women, in the industry. During the First World War she served in the Red Cross in France and received the Croix de Guerre. She was known locally as 'Meddlesome Millie', more by the potbank owners and civic dignitaries than by the ordinary people for whom she campaigned. She was caricatured by Arnold Bennett as the Countess of Chell. Rosemary, like her mother, was also a noted beauty of her day and reputedly turned down the advances of the Prince of Wales. She continued her mother's interest in the welfare of the people of Stoke but was tragically killed in an air crash in 1930.

1909 Built in 1909 the fire station was one of the last public buildings commissioned by the Fenton Urban District Council before Federation in 1910. A brigade had been set up in the town in 1859; each of the towns operated their own emergency services. Fenton retained its own brigade until 1926 when there was a city-wide reorganisation of the fire service.

1910 The North Staffordshire Railway provided a service to the Manifold Valley where people went for long walks in rolling countryside.

911 This was the year Walter Clifford came to live in Stoke-on-Trent. He was one of the leading experts in mine rescue operations in the country. Between 1911 and 1918 he received nine bars to add to his King Edward VII First Class Medal which was popularly known as the Miner's VC. Each bar represented a mining disaster attended and illustrates the extremely hazardous nature of mining. Clifford is seen here, seated, with the Goldendale Colliery No. 1 Rescue Brigade. The rescue teams operated on a rapid response basis, moving between collieries as required. Their heroism undoubtedly relieved some of the suffering felt by individuals and communities during a disaster. Between 1855 and the end of the Second World War there were over thirty disasters in the North Staffordshire coal field. The worst of these, in terms of loss of life, was at the Minnie Pit in Halmerend in 1918 where 155 lives were lost.

912 A view up Piccadilly and Albion Street from Broad Street.

1913 Sergeant Bateman on the occasion of his retirement from the force. Bateman had served for twenty-five years and had seen the reorganisation of the police on several occasions. When he joined each of the towns operated its own police force, a function centralised under the new county borough after 1910. He is pictured below as part of special force at Shelton Steelworks.

1914 Minnie Holmes in a Red Cross uniform of the First World War. The dark grey dress had a separate bodice. The rest of the uniform was a white apron, cap, a pair of cuffs and a belt. The nurse was also issued with two pairs of white stockings.

1914 Hartshill Cemetery. Opened in 1883–4, the cemetery provided much needed burial space in the borough. The imposing towers remain today but have lost the spires.

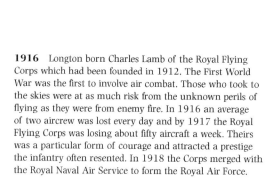

1915 Prudence Emilia Malpass. She began work in service near Endon before going to work at Ridgways with her mother. Prudence was obviously a woman conscious of fashion. Wristwatches were becoming more popular at this time and the one she is wearing is unusual because of its size.

1916 Longton born Charles Lamb of the Royal Flying Corps which had been founded in 1912. The First World War was the first to involve air combat. Those who took to the skies were at as much risk from the unknown perils of flying as they were from enemy fire. In 1916 an average of two aircrew was lost every day and by 1917 the Royal Flying Corps was losing about fifty aircraft a week. Theirs was a particular form of courage and attracted a prestige the infantry often resented. In 1918 the Corps merged with the Royal Naval Air Service to form the Royal Air Force.

1916 Private James Molam was the first member of Company 9th Battalion North Staffordshire Regiment (Pioneers) to be awarded the Military Medal. On 8 January 1916 at Pommier he carried a wounded comrade to safety under enemy fire. The 9th was made up of miners from Hanley Deep Pit, the so called 'Pioneers'. They were recruited to dig the trenches and tunnels, later becoming infantry themselves. It is the 9th and the 5th Battalions of the North Staffordshire Regiment that are most closely associated with the Potteries.

1916 George Edward Lamb of Longton was posted to Ireland. He received a gunshot wound to the upper arm during the uprising and later died from gangrene.

1916 Kitchen staff at the London Road Institution photographed during the First World War. The huge vats and brass cooking utensils echo the past Edwardian period. The lids for the vats were so heavy they were lifted with the crane to be seen at the right of the photograph. The institution had been the workhouse and was to develop into the City General Hospital.

The Zeppelins come and go, but we still keep the flag flying.

1916 A humorous card with a propaganda intent. German Zeppelin airships bombed Britain resulting in some considerable damage. It was the first time the civilian population of a country had been attacked from the air. Such direct experience along with graphic journalism and photography, as well as the return of badly wounded soldiers, brought home to the public the horrors of war.

1917   Three young officers pose for the camera in France. They were all from the North Staffordshire Regiment. Their casual air and impeccable appearance served to reassure loved ones at home.

1918 12 January 1918 saw the worst pit disaster in the North Staffordshire coal field. At the time of the explosion at the Minnie Pit, 247 men and boys were underground; 155 died. The disaster was attended by rescue teams from around the region. The photograph shows the Apedale No. 1 Team. Recovery of the bodies was a long process. The shafts remained unstable and lacked oxygen. The final body was recovered on 19 August 1919, over a year after the disaster.

1917 Tanks had made their first appearance in the war in 1916 at the battle of the Somme. They were slow and unreliable but their potential force was seized upon as a propaganda tool. Tank 119 drew huge crowds in Stoke, as did the other heavy artillery that was wheeled into Market Square in 1919. The postmark on the back of this postcard urges people to 'Feed the Guns with War Bonds'.

1918 Stoke School of Art and Library. The School of Art, seen in the distance, was built in 1858–60 to the Gothic designs of James Murray, while the Library building by Charles Lynam was built between 1877 and 1878. Behind the distinctive round windows, the building also housed the collections of the Potteries Athenaeum, one of the earlier museums in the Potteries. The card is postmarked January 1918.

1920 Eveline Coomer wearing clothes made by her mother, Evelyn. Her mother ran two babywear and drapery stalls on Stoke market from 1917 through the 1920s. She made her own knitwear for sale, always using a pair of size 9 black whalebone needles. During the 1930s and 1940s she supplied soft furnishings to Huntbach's, a local department store.

1919 London Road at the junction with Chamberlain Avenue, Stoke. The road is noticeably quiet and free of traffic. Only two motor vehicles can be seen but already these outnumber the single horse-drawn cart. Lighting is still provided by gas lamps.

1920 The Villas were built in Stoke by a group of wealthy pottery manufacturers in the 1840s. Italianate in style they contrast markedly with the usual housing in the town. The entrance to the road on which they stand was secured with wrought-iron gates, strongly suggesting that this was an exclusive area. In the distance can be seen a stepped fountain, adding further interest to the neighbourhood.

1920 Working-class housing remained basic and often unsanitary. Terrace succeeded terrace. The First World War brought about an increased awareness of the poor condition of workers' homes. Initially this did little to overcome the housing shortage which followed a war during which the building programme had virtually stopped. It was only in the 1920s that the slum clearances began. The local authority began to develop large housing estates to replace the terraces. Private house building also helped to meet the demand. The Sutton Buildings Trust acquired land in Trent Vale and opened an estate in 1929. In 1927 eight houses were built in Avenue Road, Hanley Park, that were free of gas; all the services were electric. It was no coincidence that this was also the time the pottery industry began to move towards electricity. Stoke was the first authority in the country to submit a five-year plan under the 1930 Housing Act. Labour councillors had obtained their first majority on the council and have dominated the local political scene since. The problems caused by the proximity of the industry were at last recognised. Even so, by the time of the 1935 Housing Act, there were over 3,000 overcrowded families in the Potteries. The City began to develop former agricultural land towards the east to meet demand.

1920 Stoke station. A large number of porters are at hand to deal with the carts of luggage and there are several milk churns on flatbed carts up and down the platform. The cart in the foreground displays the Staffordshire Knot, the symbol of the North Staffordshire Railway Company that had its headquarters at the station. The station has changed little since it was built in 1848 although a new roof was erected over the platforms in 1893 at which time the electric lighting was also installed.

1921 Harriet Johnson was licensed to sell tobacco from her shop (right) in Sheaf Passage, Longton. She was also very active in the Salvation Army and reached the rank of lieutenant. Harriet can also be seen on the left (below) with Captain Barman.

1922 A charabanc breaks down outside the Town Hall in Burslem. A small group of passengers and onlookers watch as the driver attempts to repair the vehicle. A horse and cart waits patiently to resume its journey. Above the Town Hall stands the Angel of Burslem, a much loved landmark of the town that claims to be the mother town of the Potteries.

1923 The Stoke-on-Trent Football Team. Not to be confused with Stoke City, this is the ladies team that won the Ladies Cup. Note the tram in the background.

In Sickness and in Health

1925 King George V visited the Potteries to lay the foundation stone of the extensions to the North Staffordshire Infirmary. This is Queen Mary, shaded by a parasol, on the steps of the hospital. On the same visit the King conferred the title and status of City on Stoke-on-Trent. In 1928 the title of mayor was replaced with that of Lord Mayor.

1925 It was Josiah Wedgwood himself who realised the importance of the canals to the emerging pottery industry, cutting the first sod of the Trent and Mersey Canal near his factory at Etruria. The canals opened up the world markets to the industry via the ports of Liverpool and Hull. Superseded by the railways, the canals continued to be used for local bulk transportation. Whole families would work the boats and a 22-hour day was not unusual even for children in the 1920s. Even so, the families were often on or below the breadline and were the subject of abuse akin to that endured by gypsies. The children of the canal workers were spat upon while queuing for bread, and boats were urinated on from bridges. (*The Sentinel*)

1926 A Potteries charabanc on a trip to Matlock on 6 July 1926. Although the railway network around the Potteries was extensive, allowed access to all parts of the country and was extremely well used, motor transport became popular. The charabanc was a common sight during the 1920s and people dressed in their best to go on day trips. (*Courtesy of Cooper-Bloor*)

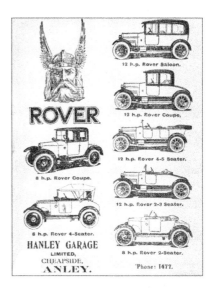

1928 During the 1920s wealthier individuals were able to live further away from their place of work. As they moved their houses became available for others and were often split into flats or lodgings. Large suburbs such as Trentham and the Westlands were built for the increasingly affluent middle classes. Those who could afford to bought motor cars with which to travel to work. In 1923 95,000 motor cars were produced and by 1928 this figure had increased to 212,000, thanks mainly to the introduction of American-style mass production techniques to British factories. In the 1920s Hanley Garage was one of the region's main outlets for Rover cars. From their Cheapside premises the garage sold a wide range of Rovers from the 8hp 2-seater to the 12hp saloon offering refined comfort. Hanley Garage was also an agent for Austin and for Armstrong Siddeley cars.

1928 Members of staff relax for an informal portrait on the stage of the Grand Theatre in Hanley. When James Elphinstone became the proprietor of the Theatre Royal in Pall Mall, Hanley, in 1873, he established a dynasty of theatre owners in the Potteries. His son Charles bought the Theatre Royal in 1892 and his other son James took out a lease on the Queen's Theatre in Longton. Charles was more successful, taking on the circus in Tontine Street on what is now the site of the post office. When the Council ordered that this building be demolished on safety grounds, Charles employed Frank Matcham to design a combined theatre and circus. In 1901 Elphinstone acquired the King's Palace Theatre and ran the Empire Picture Palace (the modern Piccadilly Arcade). The Grand was destroyed by fire in 1932 and was replaced with the Odeon.

1929 A young lady poses for her photograph in one of the numerous studios that sprang up in the Potteries. Each of the towns responded to the public need to photograph itself. Photography was reaching a mass audience, and cameras were reasonably priced and easy to use. For this type of portrait, however, the studio photographer was indispensable.

1930 Birches Head Road. Pre- and postwar housing face each other and the street lamps have been converted to electricity.

1930   A visit to Trentham Gardens could be expensive as well as exhausting. The use of a tennis court was 7s 6d for the afternoon; a trip round the lake in a boat would cost 6d; fishing was 2s 6d per rod per day; but golfing was a snip at 4d a round including clubs and balls.

1930   The wedding of Elizabeth Leese and James Blore took place on 8 February 1930. The bride and her maids wore extremely fashionable dresses and head gear. The caps worn by the bridesmaids were based on the boudoir cap and were very popular in the late 1920s and early 1930s.

1931 Hartshill Orthopaedic Hospital, 16 April 1931. Extensions to the hospital had started in 1930 when Viscount Ednam laid the foundation stone, and here Sir Robert Jones and Dame Agnes Hunt (who had worked with the Duchess of Sutherland) take time out from their tour of inspection to pose with staff from the hospital. Also in the portrait are staff from the outlying clinics at Leek, Lichfield, Stafford and Congleton. The ladies in white are masseuses, forerunners of the physiotherapists. The corner of Longfields House, now the site of the Medical Institute, can be seen on the right of the image. This was the birthplace in 1826 of the novelist Dinah Mullock who, under the pseudonym Mrs Craik, wrote *John Halifax, Gentleman*.

1932 The locally based Michelin factory has produced many specialist tyres. This is a rail car fitted with rubber tyres that have a flange allowing the vehicle to run along railway lines.

932 Between the wars Blackpool and Southport became m favourites with Potteries people for their holidays. This usual family portrait was taken as a memento in the dios of Charles Howell, the official photographer on the easure Beach.

1933 The community nurse was a familiar sight during the interwar years. At a time when it was impractical for people, and women in particular, to attend doctors and hospitals, the community nurse would provide much needed advice and care, especially following childbirth.

1936 A group of young men pose for a picture at Wedgwoods in Etruria while waiting for a bus to take them to the Duke of York's camp. The camp took place between 4–11 August 1934 at Southwold in Suffolk. It appears to have been similar to a Duke of Edinburgh Award scheme, those attending taking part in tournaments including football and cricket.

1934 Seen from the Queens Road and Hartshill cemetery side, this is the North Staffordshire Infirmary. It was built in 1869 and was one of the first in the country to be built along Florence Nightingale's pavilion principle.

1934 The summer of 1934 recorded at Trentham Gardens with the family's first camera – a Kodak Brownie. The new clothes indicate that for this family at least the depression was lifting. The older girl's dress cost 5s and was also worn at the Stoke Art School Ball the same year. It was a blue dress with pink rosebuds and for the Ball was set off with pompons taken from a pair of bedroom slippers. The younger girl's dress was brand new and cost 30s.

1934 Young men ready for inspection at the Labour Instruction Centre, Coed-y-Brenin in Wales. Unemployed men from the Potteries were sent to this camp to learn skills with which to find work.

1934 The Co-op Laundry was described by one former employee as a horrible place in which to work at this time. The hours were long – 6.00 a.m. until 5.00 p.m. – with overtime available depending upon the employee's age. The workers received 7s a week which was a good rate of pay. Customers paid 1s for twelve items of clothes to be laundered; this included the collection of the order by horse and cart.

1934 Meir aerodrome came into operation in 1934 as the base for the North Staffordshire Aero Club, an exclusive club patronised by potbank owners and other wealthy members of society. The concrete runway was added during the war for the Blenheim bombers that were assembled at the nearby Rootes factory in Blythe Bridge. Beaufighters, Havards, Mustangs and Spitfires all flew out of Meir during the war, but operations, civil and military, were always hampered by the pollution from the potbanks. The airfield closed in 1973 and local model plane enthusiasts mistakenly hoped the space would be available for their hobby. The site is now an industrial park.

1936 Connie, Bob and Edith Elphinstone in their best clothes outside their family home at 26 Wellington Road, Hanley. Like many houses in the period, the frontage was kept clean by hours of scrubbing. Even the pavement was kept clear. This was in complete contrast to the popular image of a heavily polluted and dirty environment. Living conditions for many families at this time were harsh. It was not unusual for families of seven or eight children to be sharing one bedroom with their parents in a house that lacked basic amenities and was alive with infestation. Mothers and wives were expected to work and bring up a family on wages that simply were not enough. It was the woman who often had to pawn possesions to raise the money to buy bread, fruit cake, lard and so on. The school meal was frequently the one decent meal a child would have each day.

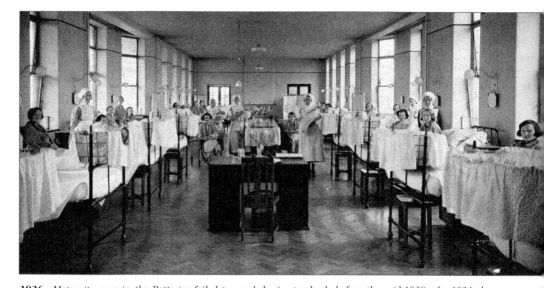

1936 Maternity care in the Potteries failed to reach basic standards before the mid-1920s. In 1924 there were on ten beds at the City General dedicated to maternity care. The ward was rudimentary with an open fire to heat the roo and provide hot water. The Corporation had bought a property known as The Limes in 1919 intending to open it as maternity unit, but it did not come into use until 1928. Here what is most noticeable is the lack of privacy, although the general cleanliness of the ward is commendable. One reason for the lack of provision was that no women held position of authority. After the First World War women who had worked in industry, on the land or in the services were force back into the traditional home-based life that had existed before the conflict. Furthermore those who tried to keep the independence and work found that it clashed with their role as mothers. Birth control was certainly not an option f many women unless they already had large families. Marie Stopes was one of the few who provided advice for wome but her books were held as outrageous and the established medical profession shunned her. It was not until much lat that authorities were required to provide one clinic in their region for what was termed 'mothers' advice'. In Hanley th was to be the clinic on Charles Street. The examples of the Duchess of Sutherland and Agnes Hunt, working outside th establishment, indicate how effective the provision of services to one section of society could be.

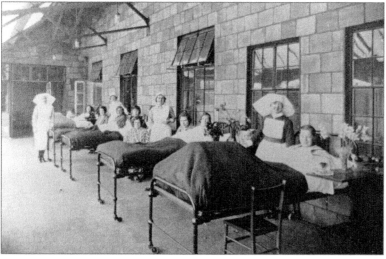

1937 Tuberculosis sufferers enjoy fresh air on the veranda at the City General. Children as much as adults were victim of the disease. The City ran a children's convalescent home in Rhyl, North Wales at a tim when that stretch of coastline was becoming a popular holiday resort for people from the Potteries.

1936–40 Minton's Pottery (above) in 1936 and Cobridge station (below) in 1940 with Moorcroft's in the background. Design of ceramics in the 1930s caused aesthetic problems that were compounded with the imposition of utility ware during the war. In 1939 the Board of Trade imposed restrictions on the supply of raw materials to encourage the industry to develop its export market, particularly with America. The strength of the dollar was much needed in Britain. The restrictions affected not design, but quantity. In 1941 in response to the loss of workers to the armed forces, the companies were further expected to rationalise and to prove that they sold up to 100 per cent capacity with a minimum of 75 per cent going overseas. This meant standardisation within the industry. The manufacturers argued that the pottery industry could not standardise its products even if companies amalgamated. The imposed utility ware was plain undecorated earthenware or china. The designs were regulated and had to be registered, given utility numbers and a special stamp.

1937 A motor cycle and sidecar on Basford Bank in 1937. The bike is an Ariel Square Four. These bikes were made in Selly Oak in Birmingham by the Ariel Works (JS) Ltd and began production in 1930. This bike was later traded in for a Morri 8 car costing £100. A year later the Morris was traded in for the same sum.

1938 A bright sunny day on Wellington Road shortly before the outbreak of war. The two ladies proudly wear the larg fur collars that were fashionable in the middle of the decade.

1939 On 29 July 1939 the weddings of two brothers illustrate the changing attitudes of the times. In the morning Jim Elphinstone married Ivy James at St Luke's Church, Hanley. The couple chose a quiet ceremony and were to go for a honeymoon on the Isle of Man without a reception. In the afternoon George Elphinstone married Nellie Jones at the Providence Chapel, Far Green. Theirs was a more traditional ceremony. Both photographs were taken outside the Providence Chapel as the first couple stayed for the ceremony and the reception.

1939 With the outbreak of war, evacuees from Manchester, Lancashire and London were moved to the Potteries. By early September, an estimated 30,000 children had moved to the North Staffordshire region. They were billeted with families – to refuse was an offence. For each child taken in the local family received 10*s* 6*d* or 8*s* 6*d*. (*The Sentinel*)

1940 Stoke-born James Williamson joined the French Foreign Legion before 1937 'to see the world'. He served under the pseudonym James Cavanagh, seeing action in the Norway campaign where he was awarded the Croix de Guerre with a bronze star and the Barrettes Norvege. It was with disbelief that he found himself camped at Trentham along with 5,000 other foreign troops in 1940. Initially the camp was surrounded with fencing and guards. Undoubtedly his knowledge of how to gain 'free' access to the park and swimming pool before he left proved useful when he sneaked out at night to the local pubs.

1940 Like the Americans who were to come later, the French changed the lives of many local people. Unlike the Americans, the French arrived with nothing: no money and often insufficient clothing. The sailor in this photograph is wearing carpet slippers.

1940 On 25 August, King George VI visited Trentham with General de Gaulle. France had fallen to the German forces and British troops had been evacuated from the beaches around Dunkirk. While arms and equipment were prepared the troops were kept on alert, including the foreign nationals who were deployed around the country in special camps. Trentham was also one of the largest convalescent hospitals in the country with over 700 beds.

1940 The treatment of traditional illnesses continued during the war. The lung-related diseases still took their toll. The sanatorium at the City General provided outdoor facilities in their wards.

1941 During the war Eveline Shore worked as a bus conductress, taking a role previously held by a man. She is seen here in her new uniform in Etruria Park. In 1941 Eveline was working in a fruit and flower shop but responded to the call to help with the war effort. She was too young to join the police which is what she wanted to do and did not want to join the Land Army. She went to the bus depot for an interview as a 'clippie', which was far from being an easy task. She was to be responsible for fares, time keeping and the safety of passengers. When she went on the longer trips – a radius of about 45 miles – she would need to know up to 2,000 stages and fares.

1943   The smiling faces of the staff of F.W. Woolworth's belie the hardships of life during the war. Despite the adversities
many women were experiencing work for the first time and enjoyed their new found confidence and financial independence.

1943   In 1927 the
Michelin Tyre Company
opened a factory at
Campbell Road in Stoke.
A major employer in the
Potteries from the start, the
firm played an important
role during the war. Here,
row upon row of military
vehicles await collection
and deployment, all fitted
with Michelin tyres. Note
the buildings in the top half
of the image have been
painted for camouflage.
Nearby Clayton Hall was
also painted in the same
way; it served as a training
base for the American
Fleet Air Arm. Today the
Michelin works remains an
important part of the local
economy.

1945 Laundry girls at the City General Hospital. During the war many jobs were designated as essential and women were employed to take these on in the absence of men. Many local women joined the Land Army and were posted away from the City. Those who preferred not to be moved from their homes and families joined the police or went to work at the munition factories at Radway Green and Swynnerton or the large clearing bank when it was moved from London to Trentham. Whatever their choice, at the end of the war women had had experience of work and made friendships and relationships that were to endure. They realised they could have jobs away from their traditional roles in the family and in the potbanks.

1945 Leivers Butchers, The Strand, Longton. A well-known local family business that also had shops in Hanley and in Cheadle. Bob Leiver left the business to concentrate on his swimming career and represented his country at Olympic level between the wars.

1945 The end of the war was the cause of great jubilation throughout the country. VE Day was celebrated on 13 May. The euphoria was immense – pit heads were lit up with a gigantic illuminated 'V'. Whole streets came together in massive parties like this outside Naylor and Nutt's builders and joiners in Coronation Street, Tunstall. The Potteries had been fortunate and suffered little bomb damage during the war. Surviving Luftwaffe maps indicate priority targets such as the railway stations, the steel works, sewage plants and the hospitals. These were only targeted if the bombers were returning from raids on Manchester and Liverpool with bombs still on board. In one such raid the residential area of May Bank was hit; presumably the Germans had been looking for the nearby steel works. In another raid the nurses' home that had been opened in 1940 at the City General Hospital was badly damaged, causing disruption to the operating schedule. (*The Sentinel*)

1946 In a pose reminiscent of the shot at the Grand Theatre, staff at the Theatre Royal enjoy a moment before the camera.

1947 Lamb Street, Hanley in the late 1940s. Taken at 10.55 a.m according to the clock, this photograph literally freeze
time. The Barclays Bank opened as all banks did at that time, between 9.30 a.m. and 3.00 p.m.; 9.00 until 12.00 o
Saturdays. A wealthy lady wearing a high fur collar reminiscent of the 1930s walks past the front of Huntbach & Co. Lt.
one of the largest stores in Hanley. A policeman watches the photographer with casual interest as an Austin car approache
from the direction of Wallis's, a store looking extremely modern and advertising its stock of coats, gowns and furs. Th
arcade boasted a mosaic floor illustrating Hanley and contained many shops and a hairdressing salon. Dancing took plac
here: old time downstairs, modern upstairs. With a pass-out, dancers could go to the Big Borough and the Crown an
Anchor pubs to meet friends before returning to the dance. This was the time when young people really began to make th
most of their evenings and weekends but before the idea of the teenager had been born.

1949 James Blore – second
from the left – had served
forty-five years at the Foxfield
Colliery and, like many miners,
wore a pure white scarf. On his
watch chain is probably his lon
service medal.

950 Between 1913 and 1950 ort Vale played at the Recreation round in Hanley. It was literally st round the corner from the opping centre. Lewis's Restaurant cognised the potential and dvertised well for the home atches.

950 Whit Sunday and the Arthur Bradshaw Band play at the Michelin Club. With Bradshaw on piano and accordion, his and included Ted Bateman on drums, Peter Stinchcombe on alto saxophone and clarinet and Peter Twigg on piano. Bands, om four pieces such as this to full orchestras, remained popular after the war.

1950 The marriage of Edith and George Price. Their wedding took place at a time when people realised that wartime austerity was coming to an end. The clothes worn by the bride and her maids were made of materials that would not have been available in such quantities only a few years earlier. The guests' clothes reflect the changing fashion scene. The Festival of Britain and the New Look are at hand.

1947 Joan Barker and Ruby Jenkins returning to their lodgings after a shift at the City General. The magnificent tower was a landmark in the hospital complex and has only recently been demolished.

1950 Park Hall No. 2 Rescue Team. The apparatus used by the mines rescue teams has changed surprisingly little since the 1920s.

1950 A view from James Street indicates the impact of the spoil heaps on the landscape.

1950 Burslem town centre. Parking is already becoming a problem.

The Postwar Years

1951   Before billboards were introduced, large 'panels' were painted on the sides of buildings as advertising spaces for local firms or institutions. This panel advertised Swettenhams, a local co-operative society. It was above the entrance to Hand Cuff Alley in Longton, so called because of its proximity to the police station.

1951 Young men trained to be miners at the Kemball Colliery which was given over to the purpose. The so-called Bevin Boys arrived from all over the country during the war and training continued into peace time. Here trainees are watching pit head procedures at the Glebe Colliery in Fenton.

1951 The centre of Longton. The bollards seem very clean and new and there is no traffic congestion, contrasting with the same scene today. Milk bars like that to the left of the photograph were popular meeting places for young people. The austerity, certainly slackening by this time, continued as the banner across the front of the Town Hall urges people to carry on saving. The image is also remarkable because of the apparent cleanliness of the air. Pollution was being tackled from the 1950s onwards with a series of Clean Air Acts.

952 Hospitals have always had a teaching role to play. This group of nursing students are attending anatomy and ~ysiology lessons in the early 1950s. The teaching regime was exacting. Retired nurses today recall the strict discipline ~posed on them by their matron.

1952 Mavis Gordon photographed in gypsy fancy dress for the Cliffe Vale Carnival. The carnival was a big event for the residents, with fairground rides, races and fancy dress competitions.

1952 Well dressing is an ancient custom that has become separated from its original meaning and significance. The date in the calendar continues to be recognised with some form of fête, as in this photograph at Endon. Troupes of dancers and acrobats were popular throughout the Potteries, performing at most major public events and holidays.

Ceramic City Choir

President :
THE COUNTESS
OF SHREWSBURY

ELEVENTH SEASON
1952 - 1953

THIRD CONCERT
TWELFTH ANNUAL FESTIVAL

Easter "Messiah"

(Eighth of Series, MRS. E. W. MONTFORD, J.P., Gift)

PRINCIPALS

ELEANOR HOUSTON   Soprano
IRENE BYATT   Contralto
RENE SOAMES   Tenor
STANLEY CLARKSON   Bass

By permission of the Governors of Sadlers Wells

Liverpool Philharmonic Orchestra

Leader - Henry Datyner

Conductor - Sir Malcolm Sargent

Hon. Chorus Master and Organist : ERNEST NASH, A.R.C.O.

VICTORIA HALL, HANLEY
STOKE-ON-TRENT
THURSDAY, APRIL 9th, at 6.45 p.m.

Programme 6d.

SMOKING is NOT permitted in the Auditorium

1952   A programme for the Ceramic City Choir performing the *Messiah*. The conductor of the Liverpool Philharmonic was Sir Malcolm Sargent. The choir had been formed during the war and rapidly established a reputation. It attracted orchestras and conductors of an international calibre.

1953 2 June, the Coronation Day of Elizabeth II. Parties across the Potteries celebrated not just the accession of a new monarch but the hopes for a new postwar era. These views of the street parties in Tunstall and in Austin Street (here and overleaf) capture the joy of the occasion. Notice the potted trees on pages 76–77.

1954 The Majestic Cinema in Stoke. The caravan advertises Lucille Ball's latest film *The Long, Long Trailer*, released in 1954. Cinemas indulged in many publicity events during a period of often intense rivalry. Many more people went to the cinema and in the Potteries there was certainly no lack of choice. Between 1924 and 1927 the Majestic, which closed down in 1957, was also the home of the first local radio station. Radio was *the* means of home entertainment. A crystal radio set in the 1920s cost about 7s 6d but larger cabinet radios featured strongly in the family home, playing a vital role during the war. By 1950 light entertainment programmes were throwing up a host of celebrities who were soon to face overwhelming competition from the television.

1951 *Carousel* was a popular musical in the 1950s. It has enjoyed many performances by professional and amateur groups alike in the Potteries. Winding the carousel itself was hard work for the backstage crew who are seen here at the Theatre Royal in their 1951–52 season. The theatre had only reopened in 1950 with a performance of *Annie Get Your Gun* after the fire of 1949 which broke out during a run of performances by the Sadlers Wells Ballet Company and totally destroyed the building.

1957 A nun supervises a class at St Dominic's school.

1957 The Wolstanton 'super pit'. It drew on reserves from three redundant pits at Sneyd, Chatterley Whitfield and Hanley Deep Pit. After modernisation, between 1957 and 1961, the pit was the deepest in Western Europe and the two shafts were fitted with tower mounted Koepe winding engines.

1958 The singer Paul Robeson visited the Potteries on several occasions and here signs autographs on his last visit to the Victoria Hall. The Lord Mayor, Councillor S. Capewell, looks on. Robeson's connections with the North Staffordshire area were strong. In 1940 a film he claimed to be among his best, *The Proud Valley*, was filmed in the mining village of Silverdale and many local people were taken on as extras. Robeson's character gave him the chance to play a leading role as an actor, not as a gifted singer. Robeson was also active in the civil rights movement in America and he seized the political opportunities of this major role for a black actor. (*The Sentinel*)

1958 The products of the industry in the Potteries often became a part of the landscape. The more dramatic examples are the spoil heaps and the large marl holes from where clay was extracted. Here, Reginald Gordon sits on a wall made from waste tiles that separated the tilery in which he worked from his back yard. In other areas of the city, dividing walls had been made from broken saggars.

1958 As entertainment the circus was in decline by the 1950s because of competition from the radio, television and cinema. After unloading at the station the circus made its way to the park in a procession. The elephants are seen here walking up Station Road.

1958 Mr Leese was responsible for hiring new miners at Foxfield for many years. He is seen here in typical working men's 'best' clothes.

1959 Piccadilly in Hanley. In the centre of this view is Boots the Chemists in a distinctive building that still stands today. In the 1932 directory this was described as the 'Chime Buildings'. To the right stands the premises of C.H. Johnson, wholesale draper. Between these two buildings, down Brunswick Street, can be seen the rear of the Theatre Royal.

960 The Sneyd Colliery in a photograph that highlights the environmental problems facing the city. Large slag heaps, the residues of heavy mining, dominate the landscape and were to become of major concern following the Aberfan disaster in the 1960s. Sneyd closed in 1962.

1960 Hanley Garage in 1960, having moved from Cheapside. An unusual photograph showing a motor bike and a horse and rider. The latter is approaching the church of St Mark built by the Commissioners in 1830. The motor bike is heading into Victoria Place. In the garage showroom can be seen a Mini: this unprecedentedly popular model had been launched on 18 August 1959. (*Courtesy of Cooper-Blore*)

1960 The *City of Stoke-on-Trent* 6254 locomotive at a British Railways exhibition at the Goods Yard in Stoke held between 11 and 24 May 1960. The locomotive was a Pacific Type 4–6–2 and was named at a ceremony in 1946.

1960 Stoke Works. Once a major construction and maintenance works, the roundhouse here is in a state of dereliction. It has since been demolished.

1960 The Palace Theatre seated about 2,000 and had a screen some 30 feet wide. It was one of the largest cinemas in Staffordshire. Earlier buildings on the site included the Dimmocks works, a huge potbank whose tall chimney had been a landmark in the town of Hanley. The site had been a roller skating rink and a boxing venue. It was also popular for dances. Granted a cinema licence in 1921, it closed for refurbishment in 1930, reopening in 1932 with a showing of *The Impossible Lover*. It became known as the Essoldo in the 1950s.

1960 Annual dinners organised by businesses, trade associations and charities are important dates in the social calendar. Business mixes with pleasure in a relaxed and jovial atmosphere at the Grand Hotel. Stan Wilcox, Ray Bould and Stephen White enjoy the moment at the annual dinner of the North Staffordshire Grocers Association.

1961 Trentham Gardens. Trentham continued to be a popular destination for a family day out up until the 1980s. Its appeal was obviously its proximity and its simplicity as well as the outdoor *art deco* swimming pool. While other theme parks in the region developed 'white knuckle rides', Trentham offered traditional games, miniature train rides, open spaces, walks in the woods, the lake and a pets' corner.

1961 The Hippodrome Cinema closed its doors in 1961 and was demolished a year later. It had earlier been the Gordon Theatre, named after General Charles George Gordon (1833–85) who was killed at Khartoum. A bust of the general can be seen above the entrance. On the opposite side of the road stood the Gordon Hotel.

1961 Pigeon racing was popular throughout the twentieth century. Prize birds changed hands for well into three figures and competition was intense. The birds were kept on allotments or in back yards, in home-made lofts. Today the loft may have been bought off the shelf. Control of the races is also now more scientific. But the 'gut feeling' about a bird remains.

1962 The Price family bought their first car, a red Austin A40. Pride in their new acquisition was short lived. On the first journey the car broke down round the corner from their house and they had to walk back under the gaze of their neighbours. The A40 was an extremely popular car throughout its production life from the late 1950s and throughout the 1960s. Over 340,000 were made in both the 1.0 and the 1.1 litre models.

1962 Hanley Deep Pit that reached its prime in the 1930s when just under 2,000 were employed on site. It closed in 1962 when its operations were taken over by Wolstanton. The site was one of the first to be reclaimed for recreational use in 1969–70. Hanley Forest Park now makes use of the levelled-off spoil heaps.

1963 The miners of Staffordshire, suffering from debilitating illnesses contracted from years in the pits, found respite in Blackpool. The North Staffs. Miners' Convalescent Home was based in the Russell Hotel.

NORTH STAFFS. MINERS' CONVALESCENT HOME
RUSSELL HOTEL BLACKPOOL

1963 The beginning and end of many bus journeys at the station in Longton. The Market Hall can just be seen on the left.

1963 On 24 April, Stoke City played their centenary celebration match against Real Madrid. The game attracted a crowd of 45,000 to the Victoria Ground. Stanley Matthews played in the match and can be seen here in action against the Madrid defence. Also in the match, but playing for Madrid, was Ference Puskas, known as the Galloping Major. It was a time when Spanish clubs were dominating the football scene and the presence of Real Madrid was as big an occasion then as it would be today. The final result was a 2–2 draw.

1964 The Apaches were a dance troupe that originated in Cliffe Vale. Seen here in practice, the dancers wore costumes when performing that were based on traditional native American designs. Their official title may have been the Etruscan Marionettes – hence the banner. They performed at carnivals around the city throughout the 1960s. Cliffe Vale itself was known as Little India, another reference to the native American. The reason for this is not clear. Some residents think that it may have stemmed from visiting circus performers. In the background (above) can be seen the buildings of Twyfords, the sanitary ware manufacturer.

The Modern Era

1968 A brief pause in work on a building site at Carmountside. The bungalows were a response to the demand for extra housing caused by the increased birth rate and falling mortality rate after the war. The war had compounded the housing problem in the city. Although Stoke suffered little bomb damage, by 1953 there were still some 12,000 on the waiting list for a council house. Prefabricated houses were set up as a short-term measure that turned into a longer-term solution. By 1961 the population of Britain was over 51,000,000 with over 80 per cent living in urban areas. Ironically over 21,000 left the Potteries during the 1950s and early 1960s, removing some of the pressure for housing. Since then, however, there has been an influx. Renovation of inner city housing has helped to accommodate these, and the City Council has promoted new developments by reclaiming derelict land.

1967 Trentham Gardens. The former Sculpture Gallery is one of the few remaining structures accessible to the public. The gardens contained mature trees and shrubs and open spaces for the public to enjoy.

1968 The Cee-n-Cee Christmas dance at the Top Rank in Hanley, otherwise remembered as the Palace Cinema. To ballroom dancers the venue was special because of its dance floor but its use as such was short lived. It was converted into a bingo hall. Cee-n-Cee was a local chain of supermarkets.

1970 St John's Church, Hanley. The polygonal apse was added to this eighteenth-century church in 1872. The organ pipes dominate the chancel and date from 1912. The church is now redundant and in a state of dereliction that contrasts with the modern shopping mall that has been the church's neighbour since the 1980s. The church boasts a unique stained glass window to a soldier killed during the Zulu Wars.

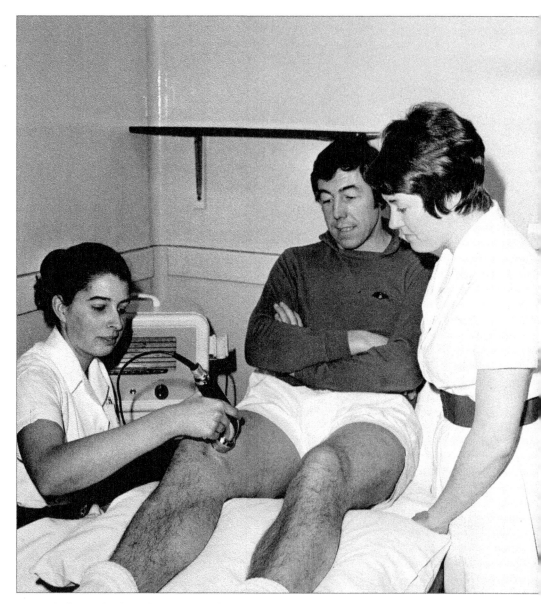

1970 Gordon Banks, the Stoke City and England goalkeeper, receiving ultrasound treatment on a knee injury. Banks perhaps one of the best remembered goalkeepers. In 1967 he attracted one of the largest transfer fees for a keeper at tha time when he moved to Stoke from Leicester for £52,000. It is claimed that Banks made the greatest save ever when h stopped Pele's stunning header in the 1970 World Cup. Banks was on top form during the Potters' League Cup victory ove Chelsea in 1972, the year in which he was also voted Footballer of the Year. Sadly it was to be his last season. In October th very same year he was involved in a car accident in which he lost the sight of his right eye.

1971 The closure of the mines and the decline in clay extraction, coupled with the loss of local passenger and freight railway lines, has resulted in a high percentage of derelict land. In 1945 there were about 2,500 acres of such land in the City. In 1971 the first earth movers began to level off the spoil heaps at the former Glebe Colliery site in Fenton.

1972 The North Staffordshire Caravan Club took its members all over the country for rallies and holidays. They came together locally each year, however, for an annual dinner and dance. The evening of 12 February 1972 was notable for being in the middle of the 'Winter of Discontent' when the Conservative Government under Edward Heath was locked in dispute with the unions. The union action involved strategically timed power cuts, plunging whole regions of the country into darkness and cutting communications. The candles on the table at the Grand Hotel were a precaution in case the lights went out.

NORTH STAFFS. SPORTING
CLUB

*Professional Boxing
Tournament*

Chairman for the Evening
Mr. DON BURTON

HIGHLAND ROOM
TRENTHAM GARDENS
TRENTHAM
STOKE-ON-TRENT

WEDNESDAY, 15th MARCH, 1972

1972   The programme for a professional boxing tournament at Trentham Gardens. The event was organised by the North Staffordshire Sporting Club whose president was Lord Stafford. The evening involved five bouts, one of which was a light heavyweight contest between Barry Clough from Stoke-on-Trent and Ade Adjasco from Nigeria. Clough forced his opponent into early retirement.

1973   Boyce Adams in Piccadilly, Hanley, in the year the business closed. The shop was a well-established grocery store selling quality provisions, wines and spirits. It also sold a range of teas that were packaged in Boyce Adams tins. Coffee was roasted in the window and the aroma floated into Piccadilly. There was a large café upstairs where many businessmen took their lunch.

1973 An intriguing image from the early 1970s indicates how little some areas changed during the twentieth century. This is the Garfield Works off Uttoxeter Road (formerly High Street) in Longton. The modern street light and the DIY shop do little to disguise typical building patterns established in the Potteries in the nineteenth century.

1974 A programme for a concert by the Tommy Dorsey Orchestra conducted by Buddy Morrow whose autograph can be seen in the top left corner. The orchestra enjoyed huge successes during the war years and performed with many of the top vocalists of the era like Frank Sinatra. Dorsey announced his retirement in 1946 but bounced back soon afterwards due to public demand. After his death the orchestra continued under the guidance of Buddy Morrow. The concert took place at Jollees in Longton in the mid-1970s. Jollees was at that time one of the leading night clubs in the country and its programme for the same year included Gene Pitney, the Three Degrees and Freddie Starr.

974 Harold and Chris Lloyd celebrated twenty-five years as dance teachers with a party at Trentham Gardens. They were ~~ighly respected by their many students as ballroom dancing maintained its popularity in the Potteries.

974 Completed in 1977, ~~ueensway marked the ~~elebrations for the Queen's Silver ~~ibilee. It is a part of the link road ~~onnecting junctions 15 and 16 ~~n the M6. Queensway, estimated ~~o have cost £26 million, was a ~~ontroversial project cutting a ~~wathe through the community ~~f Cliffe Vale and in the longer ~~rm effectively destroying it. ~~he photograph shows part of ~~alley Road. The council houses ~~ere demolished to make way for ~~ne A500 or the D Road as it is ~~nown locally. Today in streets like ~~crivenor Road the few surviving ~~ouses are sheltered from noise ~~ollution by sound barrier walls.

1977 A view along Shelton New Road. The shops seen in the middle distance near the billboard have closed as a direct result of road building programmes. The customer base was removed and the shopkeepers simply could not survive.

1978 Parker's Brewery in Burslem. One of the beers produced was known as Parker's Purge because of its effect on the digestive system. Parker's was one of the largest breweries in the area. In Ladywell Street there were 29 pubs of which 27 were Parker's pubs. In 1947 beer cost a shilling a pint, still a lot of money when the average skilled labourer's wage was between £4 and £5 per week. The brewery buildings in Lascelles Street were supposedly based on the design of the Great Temple of Thutmosis III at Karnak.

1977 A picturesque view of the Potteries with swans on the canal and Shelton church in the background. The picture was originally printed in the *Sunday Times* and was reproduced as a postcard to help raise funds for the District Boy Scouts Association.

1979 The Florence Colliery was named after the eldest daughter of the 3rd Duke of Sutherland. An extremely productiv mine, it produced over a million tons in 1988. In 1990 it merged with the Hem Heath Colliery although there had bee an underground connection betwen the two since 1979. Hem Heath had been a small-scale operation until a survey i 1947, when the mines were nationalised, realised that a massive 250 million tons were in reserve. The National Coal Boar invested heavily in the pit, making it one of the most modern in the country. In 1974 the Board announced the merge between Florence and Hem Heath, setting a production target of 2.5 million tons a year. In 1990 the Trentham Wes 'super pit' set a European record by producing 2.3 million tons of coal. During the late 1980s and early 1990s output fror British mines increased by 150 per cent, but the Conservative Government judged that the mines were uneconomical an unproductive and drew up a list of 31 pits to be closed down. The National Union of Miners called a strike that was to la for a year. It was a political action that divided the nation but one that also brought together a new community in the wor force. The wives of striking miners created support groups around the country to take part in picket lines and perhaps mor importantly, as the action struggled on, to organise fund raising and the distribution of food, clothes and money. Sudden women like Brenda Procter, Bridget Bell and Rose Hunter were taking to the platform with Arthur Scargill and Denn Skinner. They continued to fight for workers' rights after the strike collapsed in 1985. On the tenth anniversary of the stril they commissioned a sculpture in coal and stone by the artist Frank Casey. It stands in the Community History Gallery o The Potteries Museum & Art Gallery. Its unveiling was attended by miners from all over the country, a tribute to the work o these women.

1980 Hanley Public Baths were built between 1872 and 1876 on the site of a large house and gardens in Lichfield Street. The red brick building with stone dressings was very much in the Gothic style. Men's and women's baths were separate, each with their own entrance. At the time of building there was much concern about personal cleanliness and, in a town with a population approaching 40,000, there was fear of disease. Apart from the private baths, which were extended in 1912 and 1924, the buildings offered Turkish baths and swimming pools. It was a huge success: in its first ten weeks nearly 20,000 people used the baths. They were reconditioned in the 1950s and continued to be used until their demolition in 1982.

1982 The elaborate wrought-iron entrance to the underground gentlemen's toilets outside the then City Museum and Art Gallery. Such facilities were once common in towns and cities throughout the country, often with attendants employed to keep the buildings clean. Like many such conveniences these are now closed and the entrance has been sealed.

1983 Built in Victorian times and reflecting the prudery of that era, the swimming baths at Burslem were utilitarian by mid twentieth-century standards. The swimming pool was surrounded by individual changing cubicles. The pool was never deeper than 5 feet 5 inches. It was visited regularly by children who could play unsupervised in the water.

1983 A monument of stones marks the location of the altar and sanctuary of the ancient parish church of Stoke. Elsewhere in the churchyard a row of arches has been erected. Everything else is Victorian.

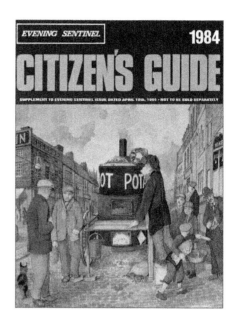

1984   The local newspaper, *The Sentinel*, published a citizen's guide. The cover illustrated a well remembered piece of the past, the hot potato machine. The machine is now in The Potteries Museum & Art Gallery. (*The Sentinel*)

1985   The army drives for fresh recruits in Cheadle. The artillery gun contrasts with the steeple of the Church of St Giles. The Catholic church dates from 1841–6 and was designed by Pugin. Pevsner describes Cheadle, a town on the outskirts of the Potteries, as 'Pugin-land'. Built at the expense of the Earl of Shrewsbury from nearby Alton Towers, the church is heavily decorated and the steeple is one of the most perfect examples of the nineteenth-century Gothic Revival.

1986 Longton Town Hall was perilously close to demolition in the 1980s. The building had been boarded up by the contractors at the time this photograph was taken. A long protest by local residents resulted in the building not only being saved, but refurbished and reopened.

1986 The Bennett family lived at 205 Waterloo Road, a road built to create work for soldiers returning from the Napoleonic Wars. The road features in Arnold Bennett's works as Trafalgar Road. Enoch Bennett, Arnold's father, was a man of aspiration and nearly bankrupted the family by studying for a law qualification. In 1879, and in keeping with his sense of status, Enoch purchased a plot of land and had the family home built. It was an area Arnold smugly described as the best end of the road. The red brick and terracotta building materials are by the standards of today not very exciting, but the features are typical to both the area and the period. This interior photograph by the former *Guardian* photographer Denis Thorpe shows the furnishings when the house was a museum. Arnold Bennett (1867–1931) was one of the leading figures in twentieth-century English literature. His novels drew heavily on his experience of life in the Potteries which he endured until a journalist's post attracted him to London. His attitude towards his home town is ambiguous. He obviously capitalised on his knowledge and experiences and became a wealthy writer as a result. Yet he admitted that travelling back to Stoke made him shudder. His visits became less frequent and almost stopped after the death of his mother. When the Vicar of Fenton delivered a sermon in 1903 attacking the low standards and morals of the workers, Bennett defended them, suggesting that the Vicar question the morals of the upper classes. (*Courtesy of Denis Thorpe, The Guardian*)

986 During the 1930s the celebrated photographer Bill Brandt compiled a huge portrait of Britain, visiting many of the industrialised areas outside the capital. One image, *Hide and Seek in Burslem Cemetery*, captured the imagination of the young Denis Thorpe. Years later, working as a photographer for the national press, he visited Burslem graveyard and was astounded to find children playing around the same graves that Brandt had photographed. (*Courtesy of Denis Thorpe, The Guardian*)

1986 The Garden Festival comes to Stoke-on-Trent. A large area of wasteland was identified adjacent to the forme[r] Wedgwood Etruria works and the Shelton Bar steel works. The site was transformed into a massive trade show that was t[o] encourage businesses to come to the city and to promote Stoke generally. After the festival the site was turned into a busines[s] park and the area in which these musicians performed is now under the Waterworld swimming pool.

1987 The Palace Theatre in Tunstall. I[t] was in Tunstall that George Barber opene[d] the first cinema in the Potteries in 1909. Barber was a man from humble origins who became Lord Mayor of Stoke-on-Trent. He never forgot his roots and once a year opened the Palace to the inmates of the Chell workhouse. He went on to open other cinemas throughout the Potteries.

1990 When the Midland Bank became the HSBC it occupied a building with an already long history. It was the site of the Dolphin Inn that was run by W. Huston who became an alderman in 1857, one year before his untimely death. Huston sold the inn which was developed into the Dolphin Hotel, and it is this building's remains that can be seen above street level today.

1995 Despite new management methods aimed at including more of the staff in the decision-making process, the traditional pottery industry continues to decline. As potbanks fail the buildings are demolished and the sites used for housing or small industrial parks.

1995 The Potteries Shopping Centre in Hanley. The mall was built over a vast area of shops and houses during the 1980s. Many local businesses were lost and the face of Hanley was changed forever. Local feeling was divided over the building between those objecting to it because it also adversely affected shops in the other towns and those who saw it as a opportunity to inject money into a declining economy.

1995 Stoke-on-Trent is a city of cultural diversity. There are Asian, Chinese, Italian, Polish, Jewish, Welsh and irish communities. In addition there is a large student population based around the University of Staffordshire and the University of Keele. The Irish community is very active, organising through its club many charitable events. In the past the *Echoes of Erin* company has performed at the King's Hall in Stoke and in 2000 there was the biggest St Patrick's Day party the city has ever seen.

113

2000 Birch Terrace, opposite the bus station, is the home of Hanley's synagogue. The Jewish congregation in Nort Staffordshire has always been small. There have been larger centres in Manchester and Birmingham that have offere more lively attractions, particularly for the younger members of the community. The synagogue opened in 1922 with congregation of 175. Today it struggles to be quorate – 10 men aged over 13. The local community is drawn from familie that moved to the area to escape persecution in Europe, mainly Poland and Russia. From the start it was a close-knit grou] conscious of its small size. In 1903 the Hanley Hebrew Philanthropic Society was formed to relieve the poor with gran and interest-free loans. Individuals in receipt of money had to be resident in Hanley for six months or more. Members c the congregation, unlike in other communities around the country, did not become involved with the local industry. Earli settlers to the area became shopkeepers: jewellers, tailors, opticians.

000 Originally intended to stand floodlit on the main A500 arterial road, *Steelman* can now be seen outside The Potteries Museum & Art Gallery in Hanley. It is a life-size figure of a steelworker in stainless steel and was presented to the Shelton Bar Action Committee under the leadership of the late Ted Smith by the sculptor Colin Melbourne. During the early 1970s the steelworks was under threat of closure, and the actions of the committee undoubtedly played a role in saving jobs at Shelton Bar and catapulted Smith into a political career that saw him serve as Leader of the Council for many years.

2000   Popularly known as the Cathedral of the Potteries, Bethesda Chapel once held a congregation of some 2,000 tha included civic dignitaries. Today the chapel stands neglected in the midst of the Cultural Quarter.

000 The Regent Theatre stands halfway along Piccadilly. It has been both cinema and theatre. As the Gaumont it as the venue for bands such as The Beatles who played here on 3 March 1963, supporting Helen Shapiro. It was after ley played at Trentham Gardens on 11 October in the same year that the term 'Beatlemania' was coined ahead of their erformance on *Sunday Night at the London Palladium*. The Regent is now a cornerstone in Hanley's Cultural Quarter but le massive development is still overshadowed by derelict buildings to its rear.

2000 The City Council considers future developments in Hanley. The Cultural Quarter will continue to expand but there are now controversial proposals to build an office quarter that would cover the bus station in the middle distance of this photograph, beyond the Victoria Hall.

Scotia, looking towards Stansfields estate. (*Courtesy of Paul O'Donnell*)

Acknowledgements

Many people have helped me with this book. They have given generously both their time and their photographs, often providing me with a very personal view of events during the twentieth century in the Potteries. The result has been, I hope, a people's history; it is certainly fresh, being drawn from, for the most part, previously unpublished collections.

In particular I have to say a very big thank you to the following for their help: John Abberley, Ted Bateman, Graham Bebbington, Mrs Broad, Lucien Cooper, Alun Davies, Graham Davies, The *Guardian*, Virginia Heath, Maurice Holland, Jazz, Fred Leigh, Garry Marsh, Ray and Mavis Marsh, the Miners' Wives Action Group, Jim Morgan, the North Staffordshire Victorian Military History and Research Society, the Nursing History Group, Paul O'Donnell, Edith Price, Ken Ray, Ian Shaw, Eveline Shore, Betty Smithers, Stoke Irish Club, Myrtle Summerlee, Denis Thorpe, Stephen and Mary White and Ruby Wooliscroft.

Many thanks to the *Sentinel* for the use of their photographs.

I also want to say a thank you to my Mum and Dad, for being there.

1900 A quiet scene in Oak Hill. While the two children appear to pose for the photographer, a cyclist disappears into the distance. Bicycles were a popular form of transport. The Clarion Club, a national cycling association, had been established in the nineteenth century to engage people from all walks of life in a healthy outdoor activity and to promote socialist ideals. The local branch was particularly active and one of its members in the late Victorian period was an enthusiastic photographer, recording many of their day trips.

First published in the United Kingdom in 2000 by Sutton Publishing

This new paperback edition first published in 2007 by Sutton Publishing

Reprinted in 2008 by
The History Press
The Mill, Brimscombe Port,
Stroud, Gloucestershire, GL5 2QG
www.thehistorypress.co.uk

Reprinted 2010, 2011, 2012

British Library Cataloguing in Publication Data
A catalogue record for this book is available from the British Library.

ISBN 978-0-7509-4899-9

Front endpaper: Hospital Saturday, Audley, 1904.
Back endpaper: The Potteries Shopping Centre, Hanley, 1995.
Half title page: The water tower at the Michelin works.
Title page: Sponging at Johnson's works, 1989.

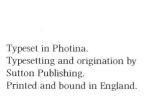

For Jan, Josh and Sam

Typeset in Photina.
Typesetting and origination by
Sutton Publishing.
Printed and bound in England.

1908 Four nurses pose at the City General Hospital. They wear uniforms typical of the Edwardian period with starched collars and cuffs.